TOASTHAMPTON

TOASTHAMPTON

HOW TO SUMMER IN STYLE

KATIE STURINO

PHOTOGRAPHY BY DANIEL BALLESTEROS

HARPER
DESIGN

An Imprint of HarperCollins Publishers

To my parents for not getting me a dog no matter how many times I asked.
I couldn't be a dog hoarder without you. I love you.

FOREWORD

WHEN PEOPLE HEAR "THE HAMPTONS," THEY USUALLY THINK OF A GLITZY, GLAMOROUS playground to the rich and famous, with fancy parties and paparazzi. Before I moved here, that's what I thought it to be. Sure, there is some of that, but in actuality it is much more Green Acres than Park Avenue. Just a mere ninety miles from New York City exists a bucolic community of farmers, artists, writers, and surfers, set on farm fields and some of the most beautiful beaches in the world. My love for this area continues to grow each and every day. The old exists with the modern in a way that is unique to anywhere else I've ever been. Where else can you see a tractor holding up a Ferrari in traffic? There is always something new to explore and experience, whether it's a great new restaurant, the latest exercise trend, a shaman conducting a full moon ceremony on the beach, or someone making small batches of artisanal cheese with six cows on a potato farm. And then, there's Toast.

When Fionula and I met Toast and her mom, Katie, it was an instant friendship. Katie and I bonded immediately over our crazy love for our dogs, and, it goes without saying, Toast is incredibly adorable. That tongue melts my heart. The pages of this book are filled with an utterly insane amount of cuteness. Toast takes full advantage of all that the Hamptons has to offer and this book is the ultimate peek into the life of a Hamptons pooch. Toast is also a rescue dog, so I love looking at her and knowing what an awesome life she has now; she truly hit the proverbial jackpot. There are so many animals out there like Toast that need homes and are ready to give and receive love.

Cheers to *ToastHampton*!

XO,
Katie Lee

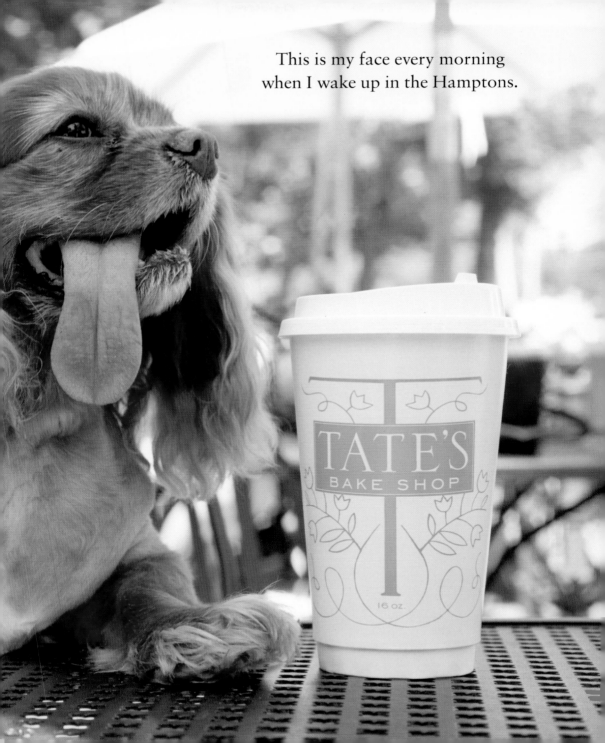

This is my face every morning when I wake up in the Hamptons.

I love to go to Sant Ambroeus
for its salad…

but…

I usually just end up having gelato.

Do you think this guy
notices me yet?

I have always been very into reading.

This week our
book group
is focusing
on the most
important genre:
cookbooks.

I actually can't read.

Who has time for traffic?

Front-row seats? Not good enough.
I attend only if I can
actually sit *with* the athletes.

Summer cashmere is highly underrated.

Sometimes I daydream about what life would be like if I weren't famous and didn't get special treatment and I was just a regular pup... actually, that's more of a nightmare than a daydream.

Late Sunday afternoons are meant
for table tennis.

A tanning butler is a must...Oh man! No tanning butler?!
Fine. Suntan lotion works better when it's applied by a
young man...usually shirtless...and of Italian decent...

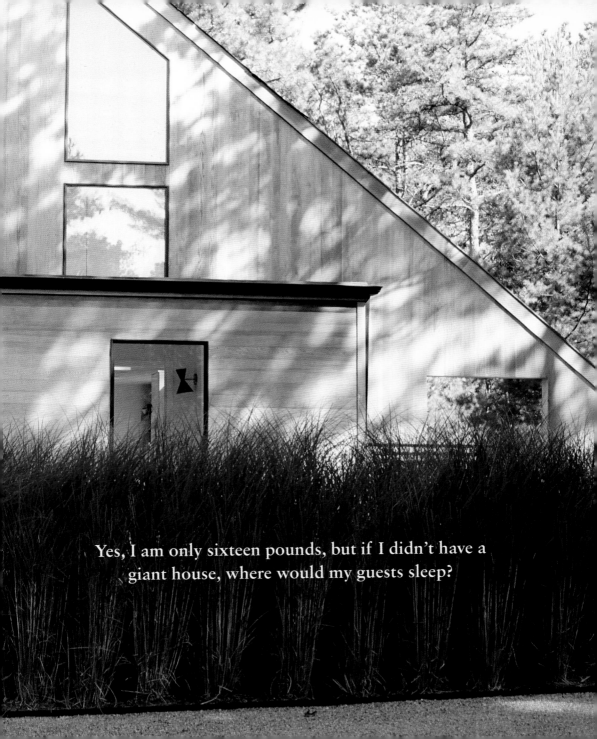

Yes, I am only sixteen pounds, but if I didn't have a giant house, where would my guests sleep?

Safari chic.

Hot dog...on a hot dog.

My colorist *hates* when I go in the pool.

Who said food is just for the kitchen?
You haven't lived until you've floated on a pizza.

I prefer to go nude
at a pool party...

Host tip: Chatty houseguest?
Never be scared to fake a nap.

My dermatologist makes sure
I never look a day over eight.

I know a great place
for whale watching.

As I always say: paws up kale salad!

Sometimes I come here to
get away from it all.

I've always been a rule breaker.

This is my horse, Teddy Skittles.
I ride to keep in shape and make sure
my inner thighs never touch.

America is so chic.

In the Hamptons, every night
is lobster night.

Planning ahead is essential...

Houseguests can often outstay their welcome...

I frequently take walks to get some space.

Culture is important in the summer
to offset the wine.

It's pronounced Jag-U-Were.

I mostly eat outside in the summer,
as I am not allowed inside the restaurants.

SOUTHAMPT
OPEN 7 DAYS
A WEEK
9AM - 10PM
OPEN
GOLF
INSTRUCTION
By Appointment
Tim McCoy P.G.A.
Reid Hansen

It's best to practice your swing before hitting the green.

Who says you can't curl up in bed
with a hot dog?

Sometimes I just have to
schedule a little "me" time...

It's ice cream o'clock
somewhere.

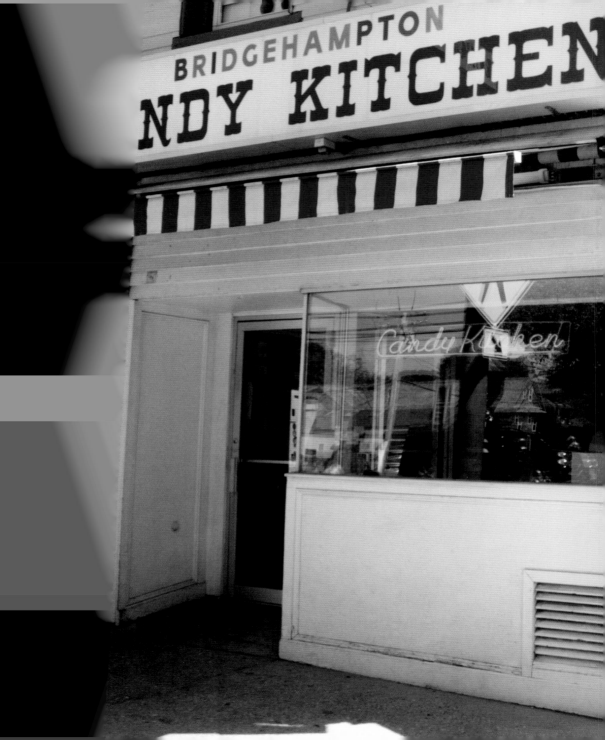

Now I'm heading out on the town!
Enjoy your summer, darling!

HEADING TO THE HAMPTONS?
GO IN (TOAST) STYLE!

Nobody has time for traffic, especially me, so I fly on **BLADE** helicopters in order to get from my apartment to ToastHampton in forty-five minutes. If you feel like being ironic (or you are poor) take the **JITNEY**. Its mini juice bottles and Goldfish Crackers make the ride fly by.

One of my first stops is always **TATE'S COOKIES**. I pick up a pack of chocolate chip cookies to eat in the car and a few to bring back for guests.

43 N Sea Rd, Southampton

For that reason, one of my second stops is always **SOUL CYCLE** or **TRACY ANDERSON**...what did you expect? I *am* a super model, after all.

68 Newtown Ln, East Hampton

The **HAMPTON COFFEE COMPANY** is all over the Hamptons, and its iced coffee is a great reason to run out and leave houseguests on their own.

I know, I know...kale salad is very 2014, but the way **MOBY'S** does it, it will feel like the first time.

341 Pantigo Rd, East Hampton

If you find yourself in Westhampton (the family Hampton) stop at **GOLDBERG'S FINEST DELI** bagels for the most delicious bagel sandwiches. Mind the side of 'tude!

65 Main St, Westhampton Beach

We love to meet our European friends at **SANT AMBROEUS** for overpriced but delicious sandwiches and to-die-for pasta—and its famous ice cream. Not to mention, we love the color palette, and its to-go cookie box is divine.

30 Main St, Southampton

If you make it all the way out to Montauk, head to **ST. PETER'S CATCH** for the fish tacos...you will thank me later.

58 S Erie Ave, Montauk

For out-of-towners whom you would prefer to have remain a bit of a mystery, send them to the TOPPING ROSE HOUSE for swanky hotel accommodations...you really don't need to see your father-in-law in his pajamas, do you?

1 Bridgehampton - Sag Harbor Turnpike

STUBBS & WOOTTON in Southampton is a must! And don't forget its end-of-summer sale if you are on a budget.

4 Jobs Ln, Southampton

Teen night at SOUTHAMPTON GOLF RANGE is a great place to toss those pesky nieces and nephews at night so you can drink in peace.

668 County Rd 39, Southampton

MESCHUTT BEACH is a hidden gem. Easy access to bay water because who needs all those waves?! It's also my favorite place to watch the sunset...

Canal Rd and Old North Hwy, Hampton Bays

Fashion and fries? What else could you want? That's why we love PIERRE'S in Bridgehampton.

2468 Main St, Bridgehampton

My friends and I love to go in to the RALPH LAUREN store in East Hampton to pick up a few bright cashmere cable knits for the season...plus, we always run into someone else that's famous!

32 Main St, East Hampton

NOTES FROM A DOGAGER:
TIPS ON DOG ADOPTION

I WANT TO ADOPT BUT I DON'T WANT TO GO TO A SHELTER.

OK. Rude. But these days adopting a dog can be as easy as shopping for shoes online. With resources like petfinder.com or adoptapet.com, you can search by breed size or age. Remember, if you are looking for a specific type of dog, you will have to be patient in your search.

BUT I WANT ONLY A PUPPY.

Why? Puppies need a year of solid training. They chew your shoes and require housetraining. It also takes a while for their personality to come out. That sweet cuddly little baby puppy can turn into a yapping nightmare if you do not dedicate the time to their training.

Older dogs know who they are (and therefore you do too!). Oftentimes they do not require as much housetraining and, depending on the breed, need less exercise.

I REALLY WANT TO HELP A PUPPY-MILL DOG

Of course you do! Organizations like these are on the ground pulling dogs out of horrible mill situations and often help adopt them out:

http://milldogrescue.org/

or

http://k9millrescue.org/

or

http://www.animalleague.org/

Please keep in mind that 99.999999999% of all pet store dogs come from puppy mills. This includes online shops and any breeder who will ship you a dog without meeting you in person.

ACKNOWLEDGMENTS

My agent, Alyssa Rueben, for seeing my vision and working with me.

Scott Munson, thank you for your photoshop magic and for all of the work you put into this book and into Toast's feed for the past two years. You are the best.

Lily Berg and Team Toast—for never/always taking me seriously. Love you.

Instagram—for your app.

North Shore Animal League, Friends of Finn, and National Mill Dog Rescue for your tireless work with rescuing dogs from puppy mills.

Leandra Medine, Eva Chen, Ben Lyons, Karen Walker, Chris Benz, Prabal Gurung, the good people of Soul Cycle, and Jonathan Adler for taking a chance on an unknown pup and posting photos of me when I had a small following.

My sister for being the most affordable CFO in the business. You also make a great intern, and I don't know what I would do without you.

Rebecca Hunt, my editor, for holding my hand through literally every step of this book to make sure it gets done. And for

snapping awkward candids of me during the shoot.

Teddy Skittles, thank you for introducing me to the Hamptons and for allowing me to hoard dogs. I love you.

Molly Borman for making it possible for me to leave the city, ever. And for your undying love for dogs and the internet.

Gordon Stevenson, Susan Stevenson, and Rick Woodward for hosting me so many times and for letting us shoot with Andy.

Dr. Karen Gilmore, thank you for introducing me to concord grapes, freezer cookies, young pecorino, the idea that it's never too late in the night to work out, and the Penguin. And most of all for being a family to me. (Notice you were not thanked, Mitchell.)

Muppet, even though you came into our hearts first, you ended up playing second fiddle. No one does it better or with more humor than you.

Pants, you make me smile everyday.

Toast, you changed my life and made all of my dreams come true.

Published in 2016 by
Harper Design
An Imprint of HarperCollins*Publishers*
195 Broadway
New York, NY 10007
Tel: (212) 207-7000
Fax: (855) 746-6023
harperdesign@harpercollins.com
www.hc.com

Distributed throughout the world by
HarperCollins Publishers
195 Broadway
New York, NY 10007

ISBN 978-0-06-244217-8
Library of Congress Control Number 2015959437

Printed in China
First Printing, 2016

KATIE STURINO Dogager, publicist, puppy-mill activist, and body-image advocate Katie Sturino helps Toast type on Instagram. She is also mom to @toastmeetsworld's fellow puppy-mill rescue dogs @muppetsrevenge and @underpantsthedog. Katie is no stranger to the world of social media and launched her own site, The12ish-Style, in 2015. She lives in New York City.

TOAST Once a former breeding mom in a puppy mill in North Carolina, Toast's face now appears in high fashion publications around the globe, most recently as the face of Karen Walker's Spring 2015 eyewear campaign. When she's not on set, Toast hangs out with Karlie Kloss, barks at birds, and spoons with her less-than-famous sisters, Muppet and Pants.